PRO

PHOTOGRAPHY

on a

TIGHT

BUDGET

This is not a basic photography tutorial book.

....

Do you believe you can create stunning photos that deeply impress viewers without needing expensive photography equipment?

If the answer is "Yes", then this book is for you!

"High-End Photography on a Minimalist Budget" is not a basic photography tutorial book. We won't delve into aperture, shutter speed, or ISO. Instead, we'll join you in breaking down equipment barriers, uncovering the hidden power within ordinary cameras/phones, and conquering the pinnacle of photography through your own creativity and passion.

In this book, you will:

- **Be inspired by success stories:** Meet talented photographers who have produced outstanding work with just affordable equipment, proving that limitations lie in mindset, not in "gear."

- **Uncover "golden" secrets:** Learn how to maximize the potential of your current camera/phone, utilizing natural light, unique shooting angles, and inexpensive accessories to create impressive photos.

- **Cultivate creative thinking:** Transcend rigid rules, seek out the hidden beauty in everyday life, and express your unique personality through each frame.

- **Connect with the community:** Access free online resources and a passionate community of photographers where you can learn, share, and grow together.

"High-End Photography on a Minimalist Budget" is a powerful affirmation that anyone can become a photographer, as long as they possess passion, creativity, and the desire to conquer. Embark on this journey with us to conquer the heights of photography, where the only limit is your imagination!

Part 1: The Mindset of Photography: Transcending Equipment Limits

Chapter 1: Photography is Not a "Gear" Race

1.1 The Psychology of "The More Expensive the Equipment, the Better the Photos"

When entering the passionate world of photography, it's not uncommon to encounter the mentality of "the more expensive the equipment, the better the photos." Full-frame or medium format cameras, large lenses with top-notch optical quality, and lightning-fast focusing capabilities always offer an irresistible appeal. Review videos and articles with sky-high praise can make users feel lost in a maze, leading those who own such equipment to believe that simply holding it will produce amazing photos.

Undeniably, expensive equipment brings certain differences, but can an expensive camera truly transform an ordinary person into a talented photographer?

1.2 Psychological "Traps" and Misconceptions

The mentality of equipment worship in photography can lead users to harmful misconceptions:

- **Misconception about image quality:** Many people mistakenly believe that an expensive camera and lens, capable of capturing high-resolution images with excellent sharpness, a wide ISO range, and good noise reduction, will automatically produce beautiful photos. They forget that the most crucial factor in photography is shooting technique, lighting, composition, capturing the moment, and conveying emotion.

- **Misconception about skills:** Owning "impressive" equipment doesn't equate to mastering it or possessing good photography skills. Skills require extensive practice, accumulated through hands-on experience and time.

- **Misconception about creativity:** Cameras, lenses, filters, tripods... are merely tools. Utilizing them creatively depends on the photographer's mindset and perspective. An ordinary camera or an inexpensive phone can create unique and memorable photos if the photographer knows how to exploit their potential.

- **Misconception about self-worth:** Some individuals enter photography by investing heavily in equipment, equating it with status, rather than genuine passion or love for the art. This not only leads to waste but also transforms you from a Photographer into a "Camera Owner."

Famous Photographers Create Masterpieces with Simple Equipment

The decades-long history of modern photography has proven that classic, masterpiece photos aren't always created with the most advanced equipment.

Many legendary photographers have used simple, even rudimentary cameras – cameras that were 10-20 years behind the technology of their time. Yet, they still captured historical moments and created artistic works that touch people's hearts.

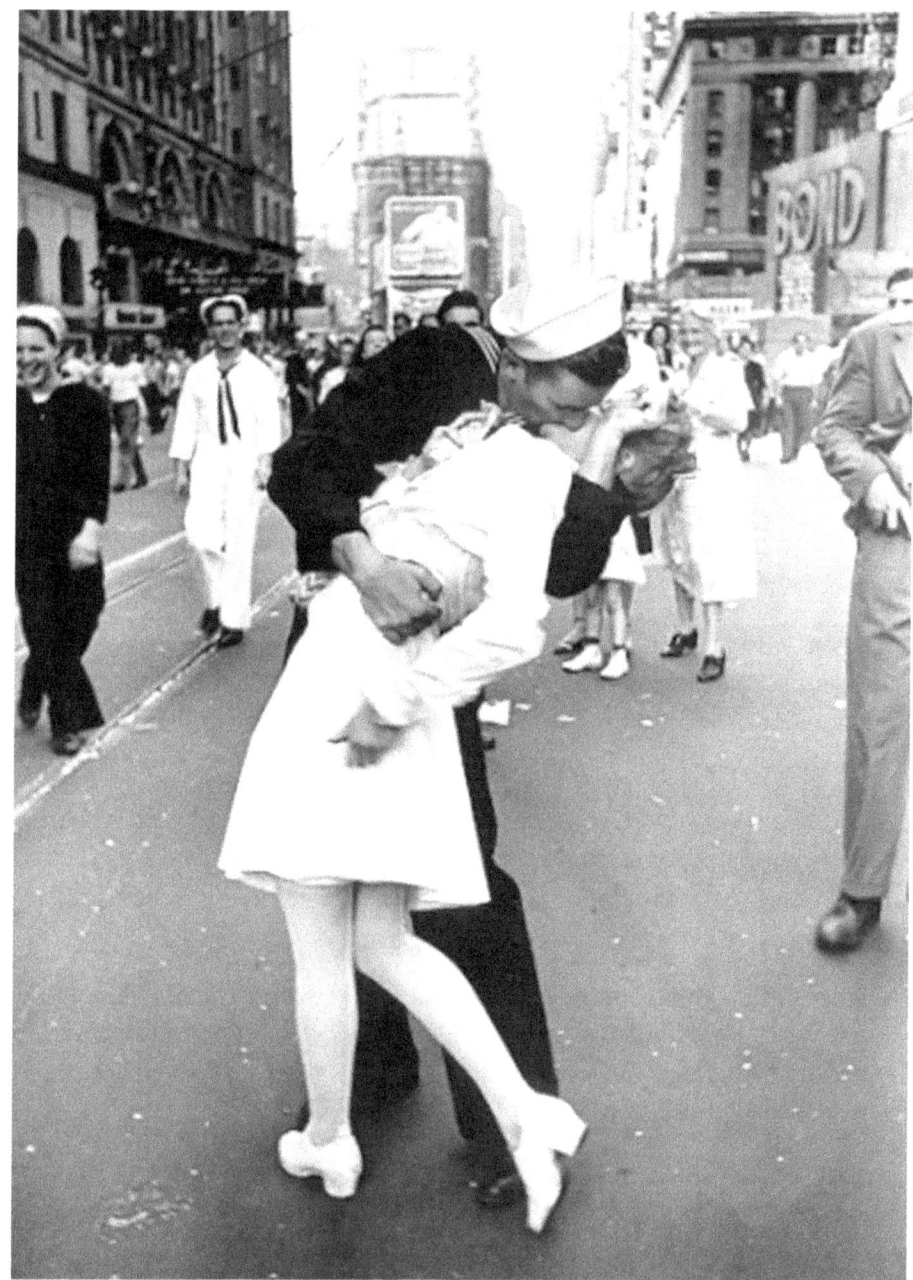

The photograph "V-J Day in Times Square", also known as "The Kiss", is one of the most iconic images of the 20th century, captured by photographer Alfred Eisenstaedt on August 14, 1945. The photo captures the moment a US sailor kisses a nurse in a celebratory embrace upon hearing the news of Japan's surrender, ending World War II.

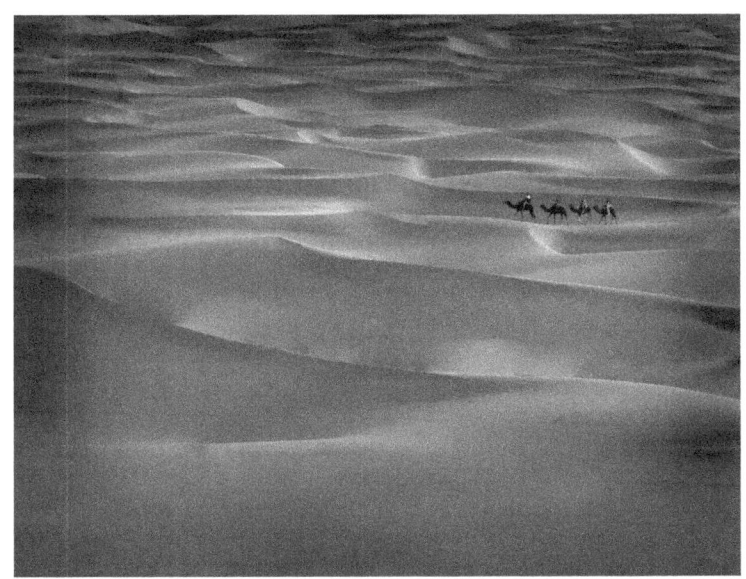

Sahara Surfing" by Khalid Mahmood (Sweden).

First Place – Iphone Photography Awards 2024, Travel. Shot on iPhone

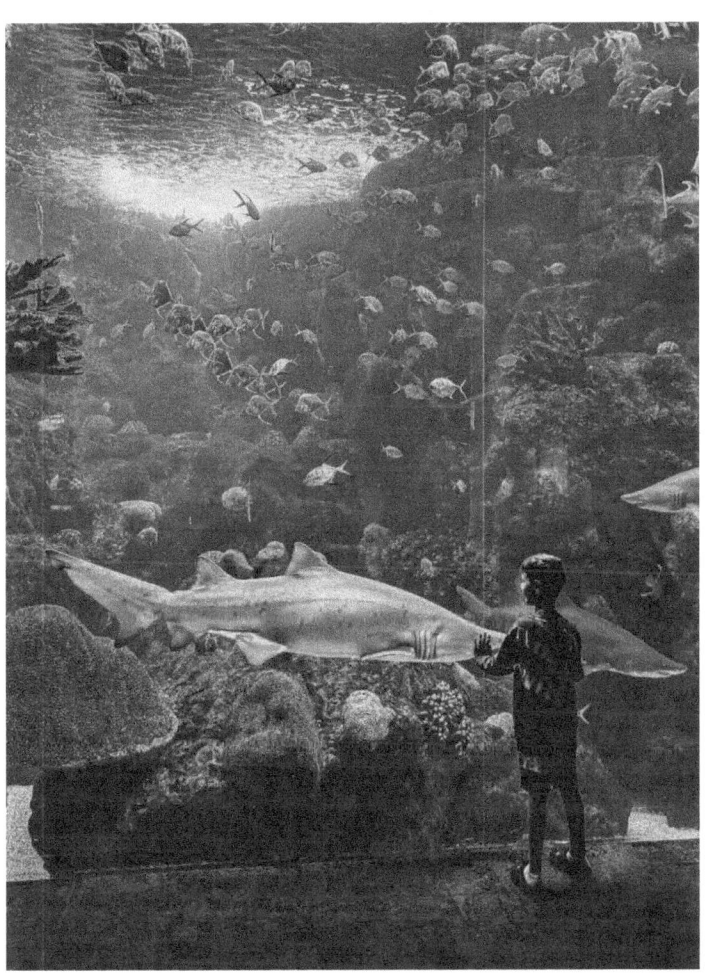

"Boy Meets Sharks" by Erin Brooks (USA).

Grand Prize Winner - Iphone Photography Awards 2024. Shot on iPhone

Focus on Core Elements: Light, Composition, Moment, Emotion

Instead of getting caught up in the equipment race, focus on the most essential aspects of photography:

- **Light:** Photography is a play of light. Learn to observe and control light, so both natural and artificial light become your tools.

- **Composition:** Some schools of thought suggest that composition isn't critical. However, to break the rules effectively, you must first master the fundamentals of composition. This allows you to create unique shooting angles and truly impressive photos.

- **Moment:** Moments are fleeting and never return. Therefore, cultivate your observation skills, be sensitive to beautiful moments, master your existing equipment, and use it to create meaningful photos.

- **Emotion:** A photo devoid of emotion, regardless of how good the lighting and composition may be, remains a soulless image. Express your emotions and stories through your unique perspective.

Remember: The best camera is the camera you have.

Chapter 2: Exploiting the Full Potential of Your Existing Equipment

Owning expensive equipment may not be as crucial as understanding and maximizing the capabilities of your current camera or phone.

2.1 Know Yourself and Your Enemy, A Hundred Battles You Will Win

Before embarking on your photography journey, it's wise to thoroughly understand your "companion." Carefully read the user manual, explore the features, shooting modes, and technical specifications of your camera or phone.

For cameras:

- **Explore shooting modes:** Beyond the automatic mode (Auto), experiment with semi-automatic modes like Aperture Priority (Av) or Shutter Priority (Tv), or even delve into the fully Manual mode (M) to control aperture, shutter speed, and ISO.

- **Master the technical specifications:** A solid understanding of the sensor, resolution, ISO range, continuous shooting speed, and focusing system will empower you to maximize your camera's potential.

- **Discover special features:** Many cameras offer useful features such as panorama mode, HDR, and time-lapse. Experiment with these and apply them in suitable situations.

For phones:

- **Explore camera apps:** Default camera apps on phones often have hidden features like Pro mode (for manual control), RAW shooting, and manual parameter adjustments.

- **Utilize supporting apps:** Install additional professional photography apps like Camera FV-5, Open Camera, or ProCam X to gain more control and options.

- **Upgrade software:** Keep your operating system and camera app updated to the latest versions to improve image quality and access new features.

2.2 Overcoming Equipment Limitations with Technique

2.2.1 Light - The "Magician" of Photography

- **Maximize natural light:** Observe and choose the time of day with beautiful lighting conditions for your photos, such as during the "golden hour" or "blue hour."

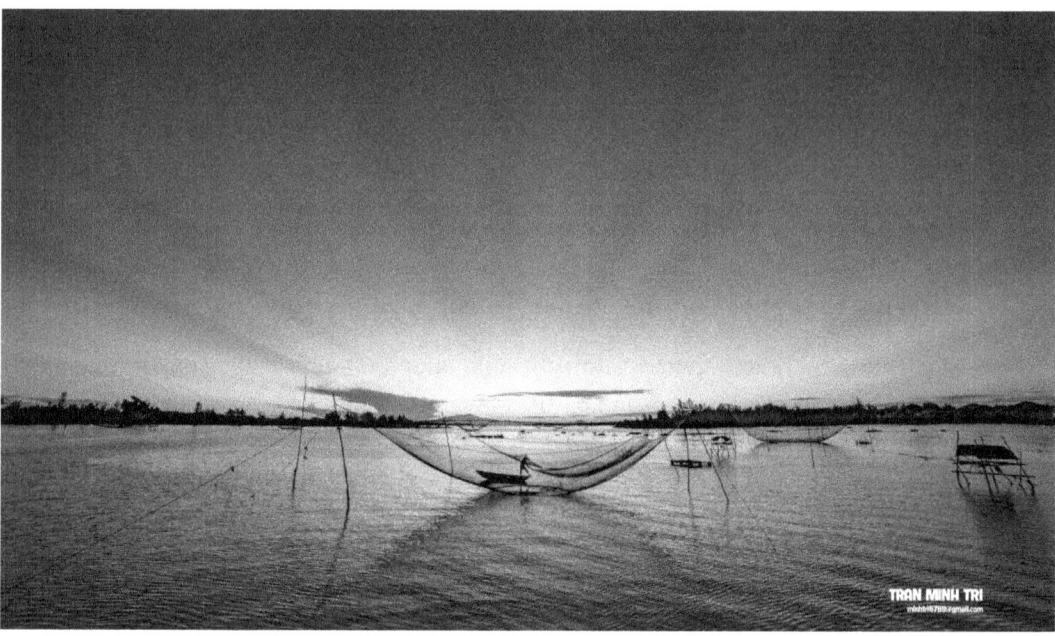

The color of the net - Tran Minh Tri

- **Actively adjust the light:** Utilize simple objects like a homemade reflector or similar DIY tools (white cardboard, white cloth) to reflect light and achieve the desired effect.

- **Play with shadows:** Shadows can create striking and artistic photos. Experiment with backlight and silhouette photography to produce unique works.

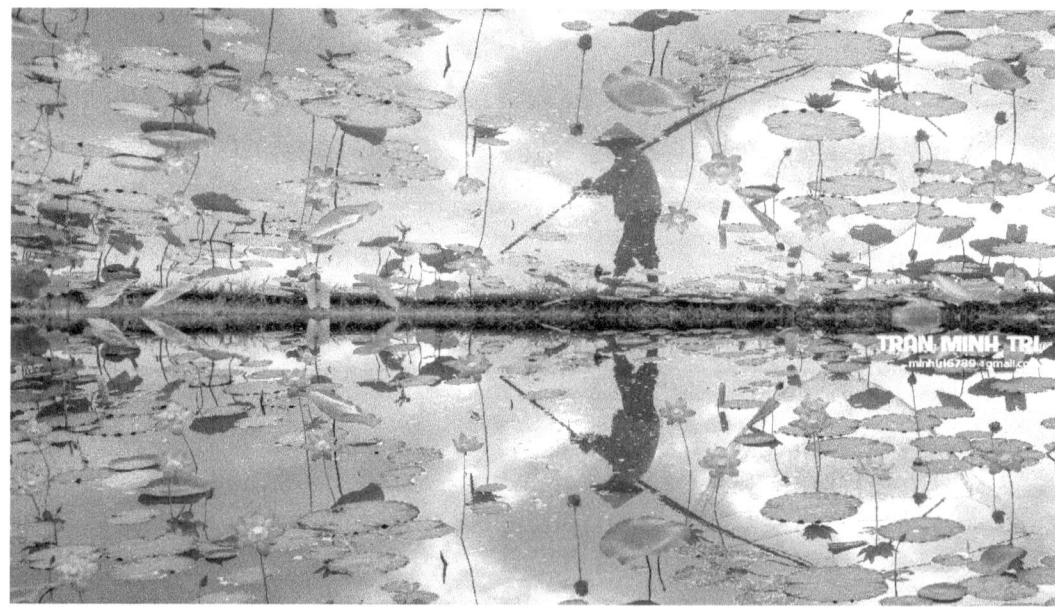

The Shadows - Tran Minh Tri

2.2.2 Shooting Angle - The Versatile "Lens"

- **Break free from conventional angles:** Instead of just shooting at eye level, explore different perspectives like low angles, high angles, and tilted angles to create fresh compositions.

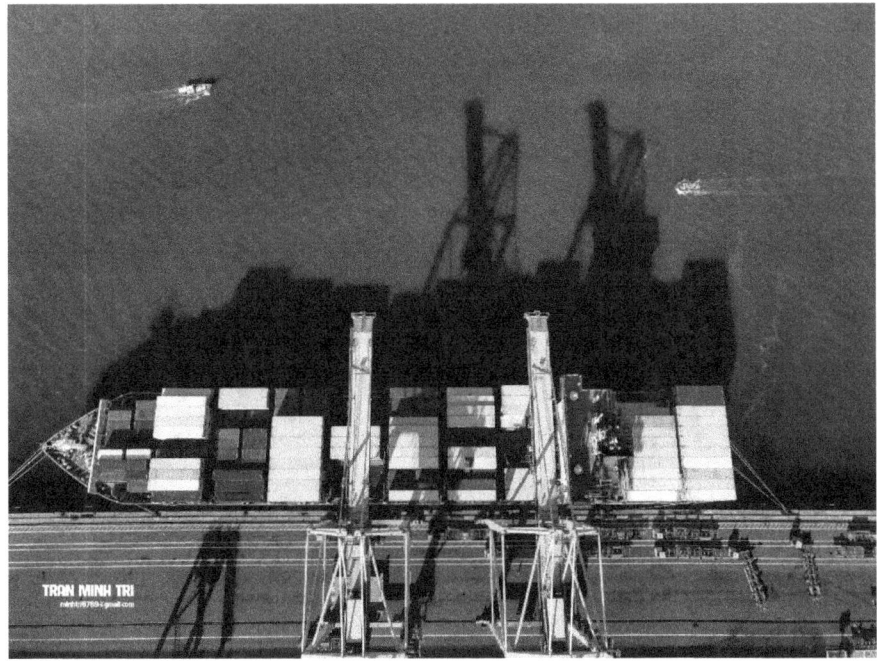

- **Seek unique viewpoints:** Observe your surroundings and discover interesting, unexpected angles to add a distinctive touch to your photos.

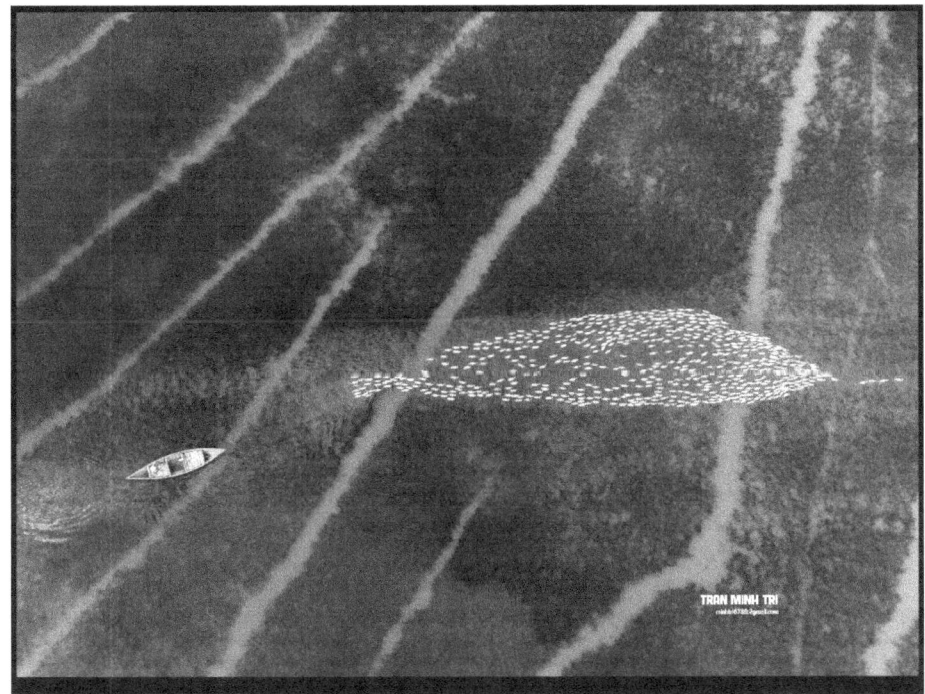

2.2.3 Shooting Modes - Hidden "Secrets"

- **Explore special shooting modes:** Go beyond Auto mode and experiment with other modes like Sports mode, Night mode, or Bulb mode (for long exposures).

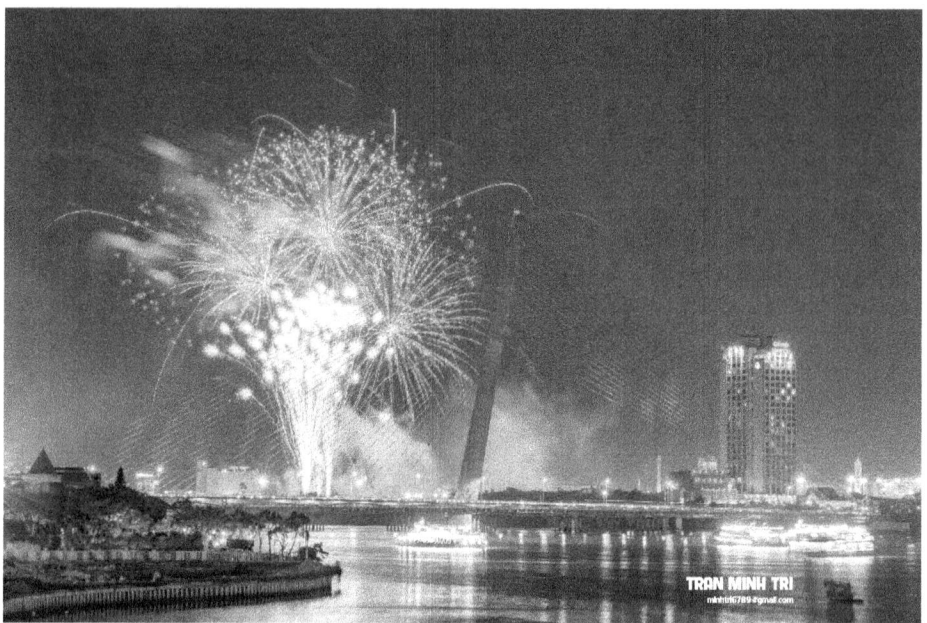

- **Combine shooting modes:** For example, combine Continuous Shooting mode with Tracking Focus mode to capture moving subjects effectively.

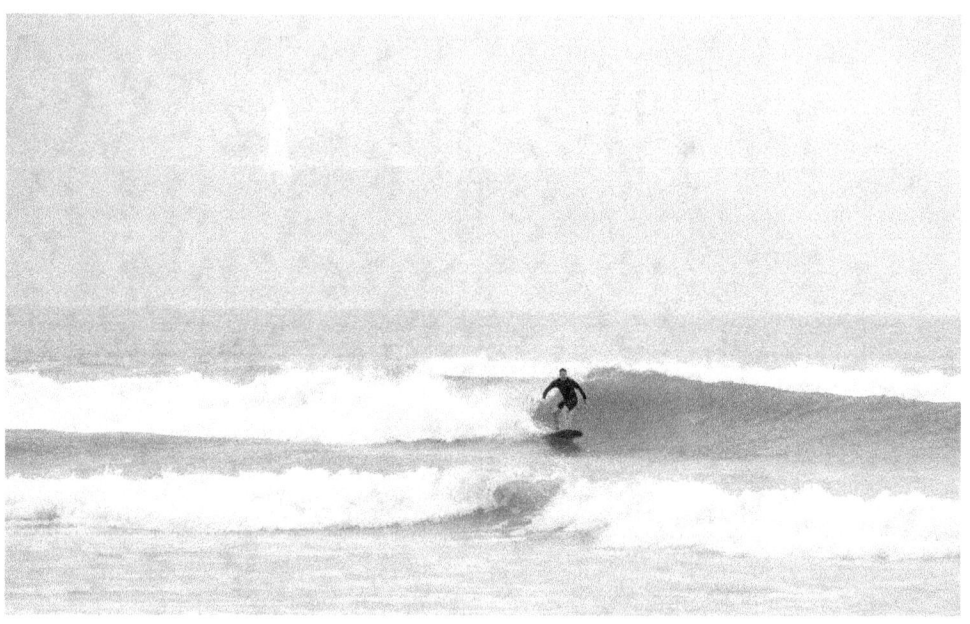

2.3 Tiny Accessories - Huge Impact

You don't need to invest in expensive accessories. With just a few compact, affordable items, you can significantly enhance the quality of your photos:

- **Mini tripod:** Helps stabilize your camera, allowing you to shoot long exposures and capture sharp images in low-light conditions without camera shake.

- **DIY reflector:** Use it to bounce light, creating a soft, natural lighting effect.

- **DIY filter:** Create your own filters using cellophane or other materials to add unique color effects to your photos.

- **Remote shutter release:** Enables you to take photos remotely, preventing camera shake when pressing the shutter button.

Remember, your creativity and skills are the deciding factors. By understanding your existing equipment, utilizing techniques effectively, and employing simple accessories, you can absolutely create "high-end" photos without spending a fortune.

Chapter 3: "Hunting" for Beautiful Moments Without Spending a Fortune

Photography is not merely about capturing images; it's a journey of discovering the hidden beauty in life. And the wonderful thing is, you don't need to travel to far-off lands or invest in expensive equipment to find these beautiful moments. They exist all around us, waiting for a keen "photographer's eye" to uncover and capture them.

3.1 Cultivating the "Photographer's Eye"

The "photographer's eye" isn't something you're born with; it needs to be nurtured through observation, perception, and experience.

- **Observation:** Develop the habit of observing everything around you with a fresh perspective. Pay attention to light, composition, colors, shapes, lines, and textures. Seek out unique elements and intriguing details that others often overlook.

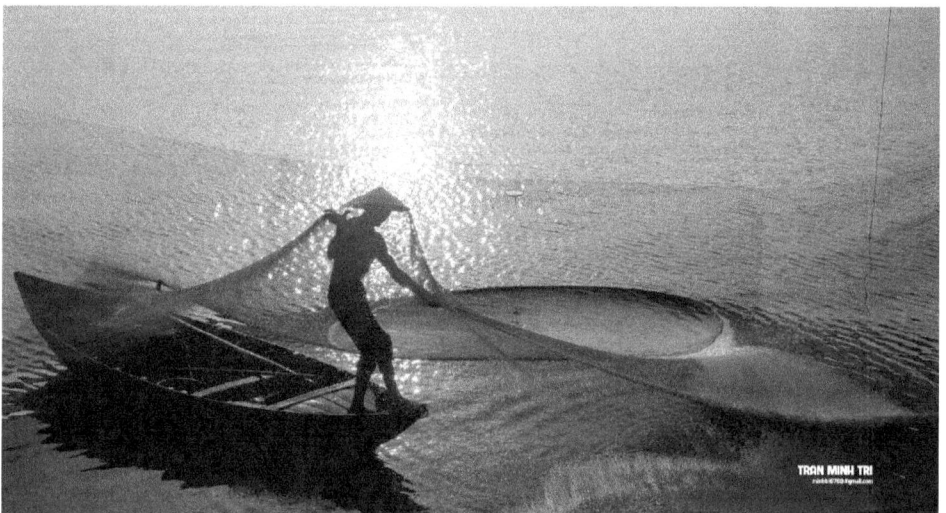

- **Perception:** Don't just observe with your eyes; feel with your heart. Look for moments that evoke emotions within you, for stories hidden within everyday life.

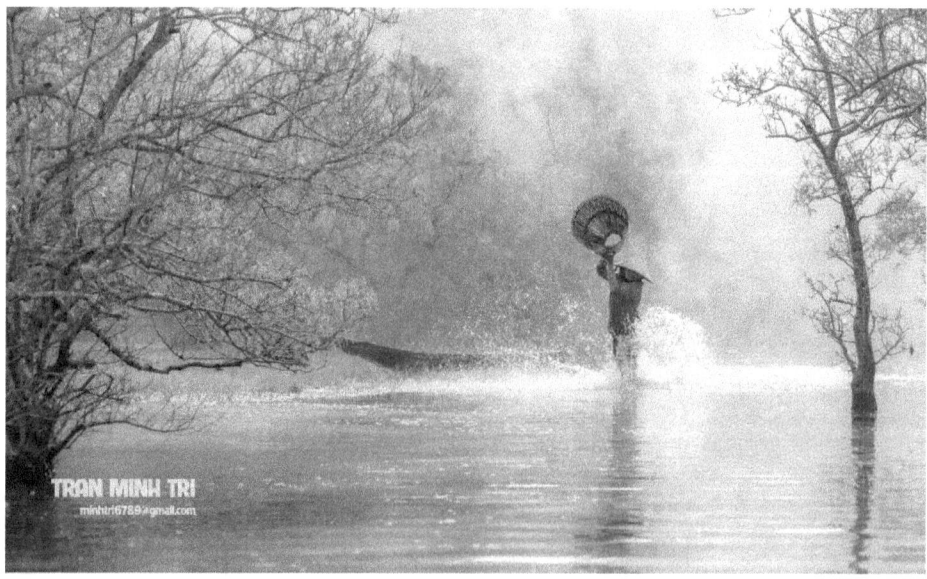

- **Capturing the moment:** Beautiful moments often arrive unexpectedly and vanish quickly. Always be ready with your camera or phone to capture those memorable moments.

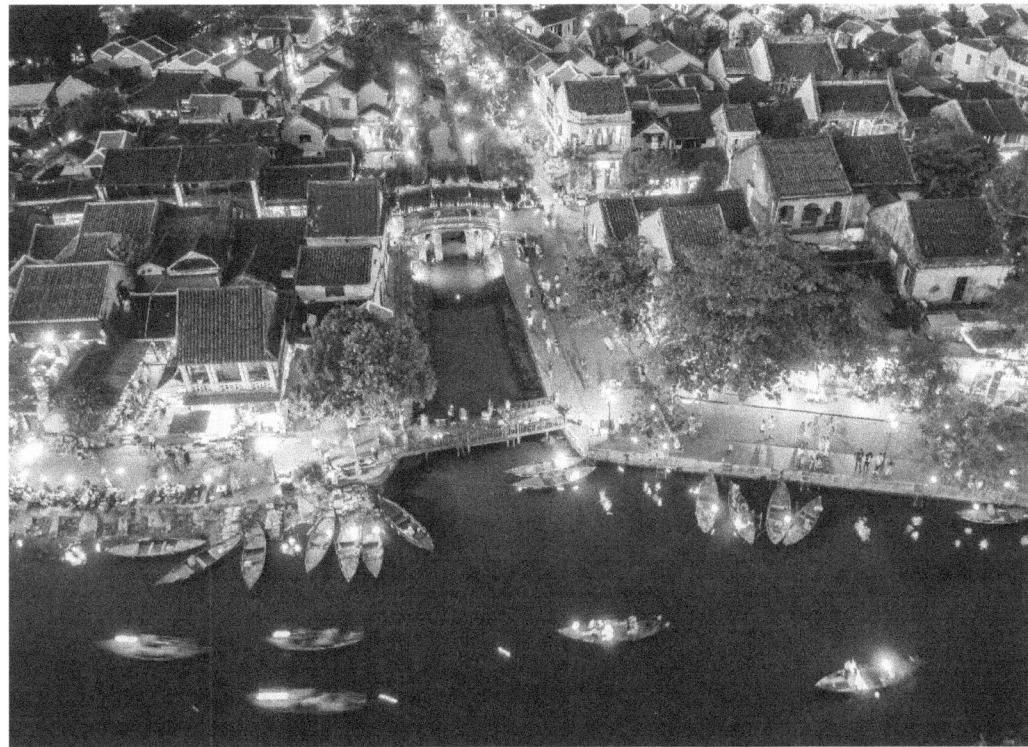

3.2 Hidden Beauty in Everyday Life

Sometimes, we get caught up in searching for grand landscapes and famous landmarks, forgetting that beauty exists right in the midst of our everyday lives.

- **Familiar street corners:** Those familiar streets and corners can suddenly transform through the lens of a camera. Try changing your perspective, paying attention to details, and you'll discover fascinating things you've never noticed before.

-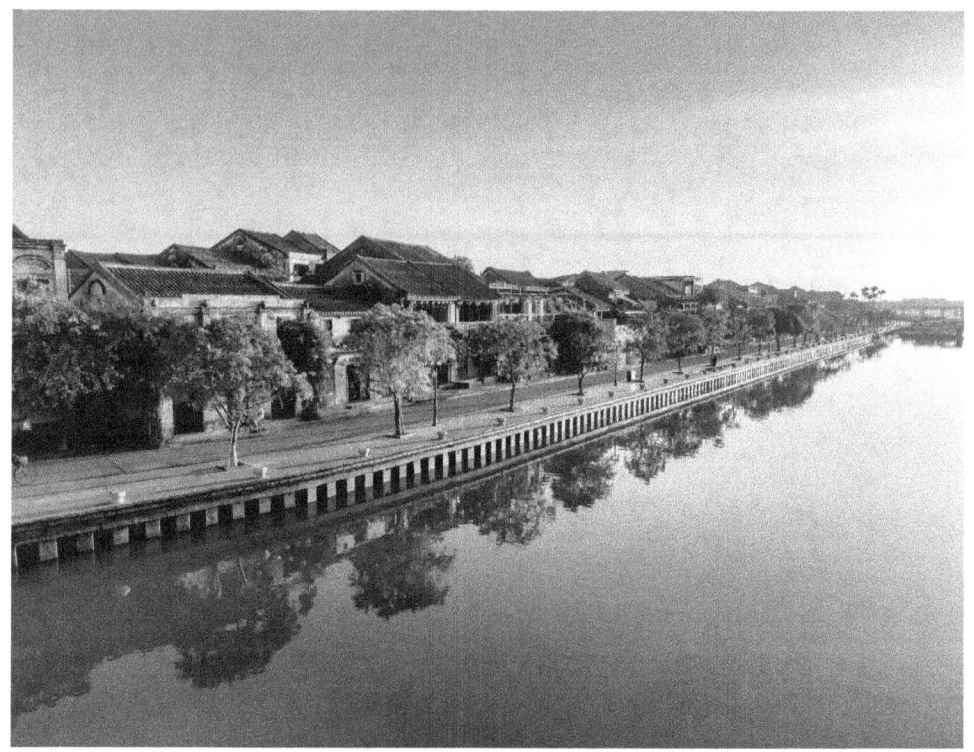
- **People:** Each person carries a unique beauty, a unique story. Observe and capture the genuine, natural moments of the people around you: the smile of a child, the gaze of an elderly person, the activities of daily life.
-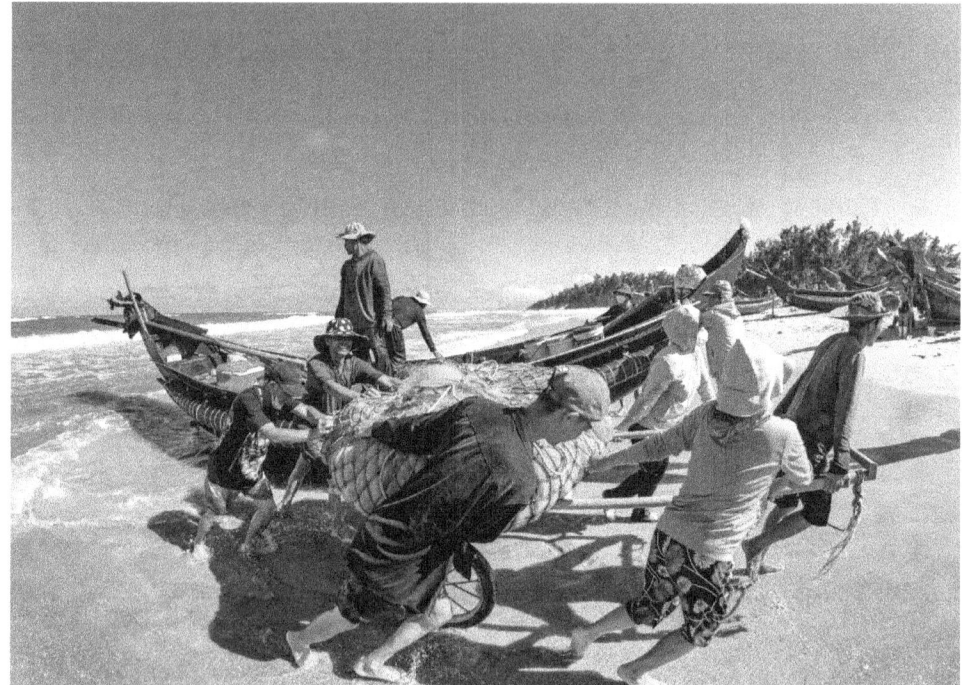

- **Nature:** Nature is an endless source of inspiration for photography. You don't need to travel far; you can find the beauty of nature in a nearby park, by the riverbank, or even in your own small garden.

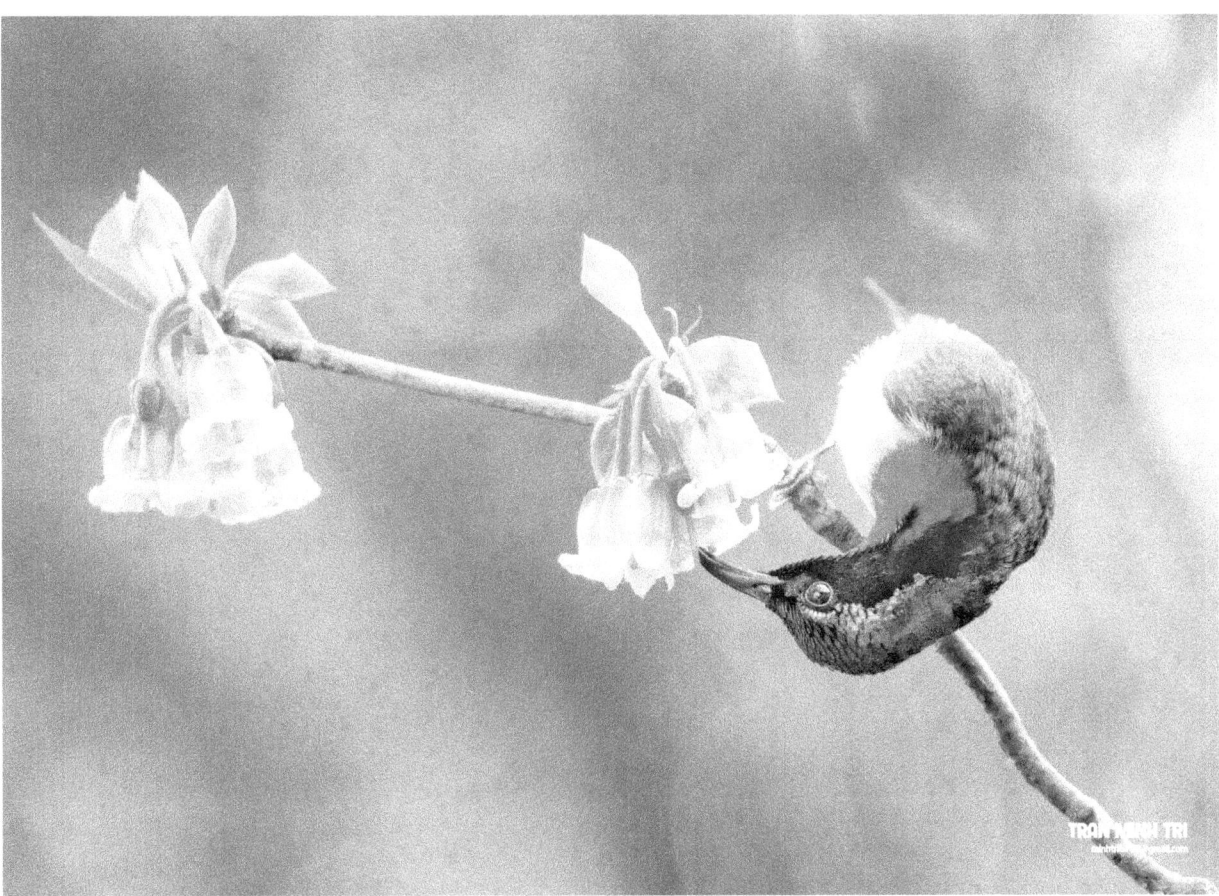

3.3 Photography Themes That Don't Break the Bank

There are countless captivating photography themes you can explore without spending a lot of money:

- **Everyday life photography:** Capture moments of everyday life, the ordinary activities of people, creating authentic and emotionally rich photos.

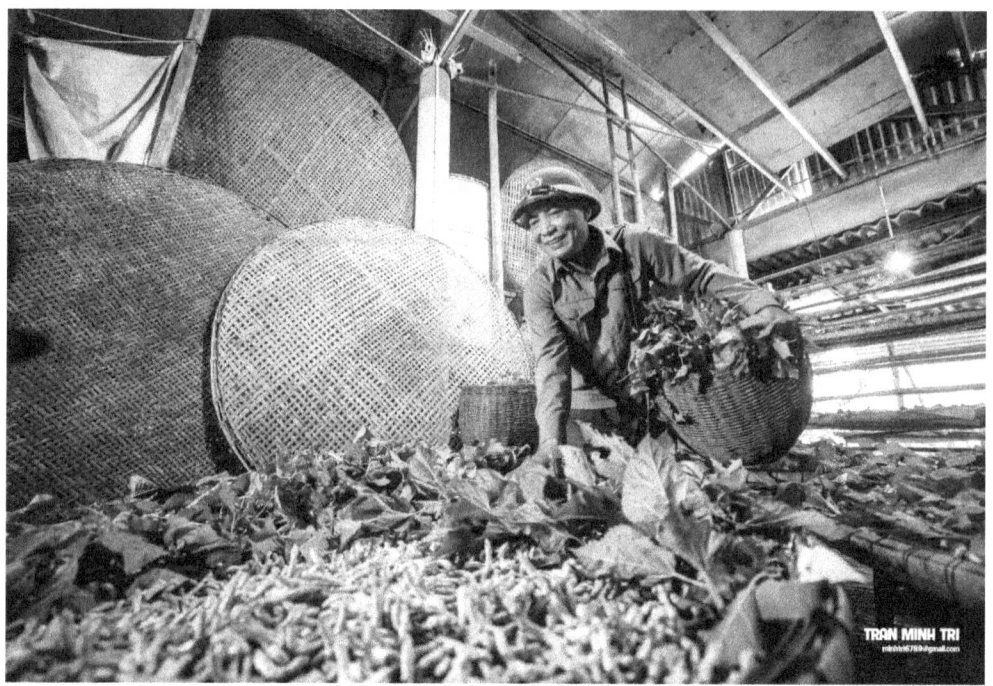

- **Abstract photography:** Seek out unique shapes, lines, and colors to create abstract images that stimulate the viewer's imagination.

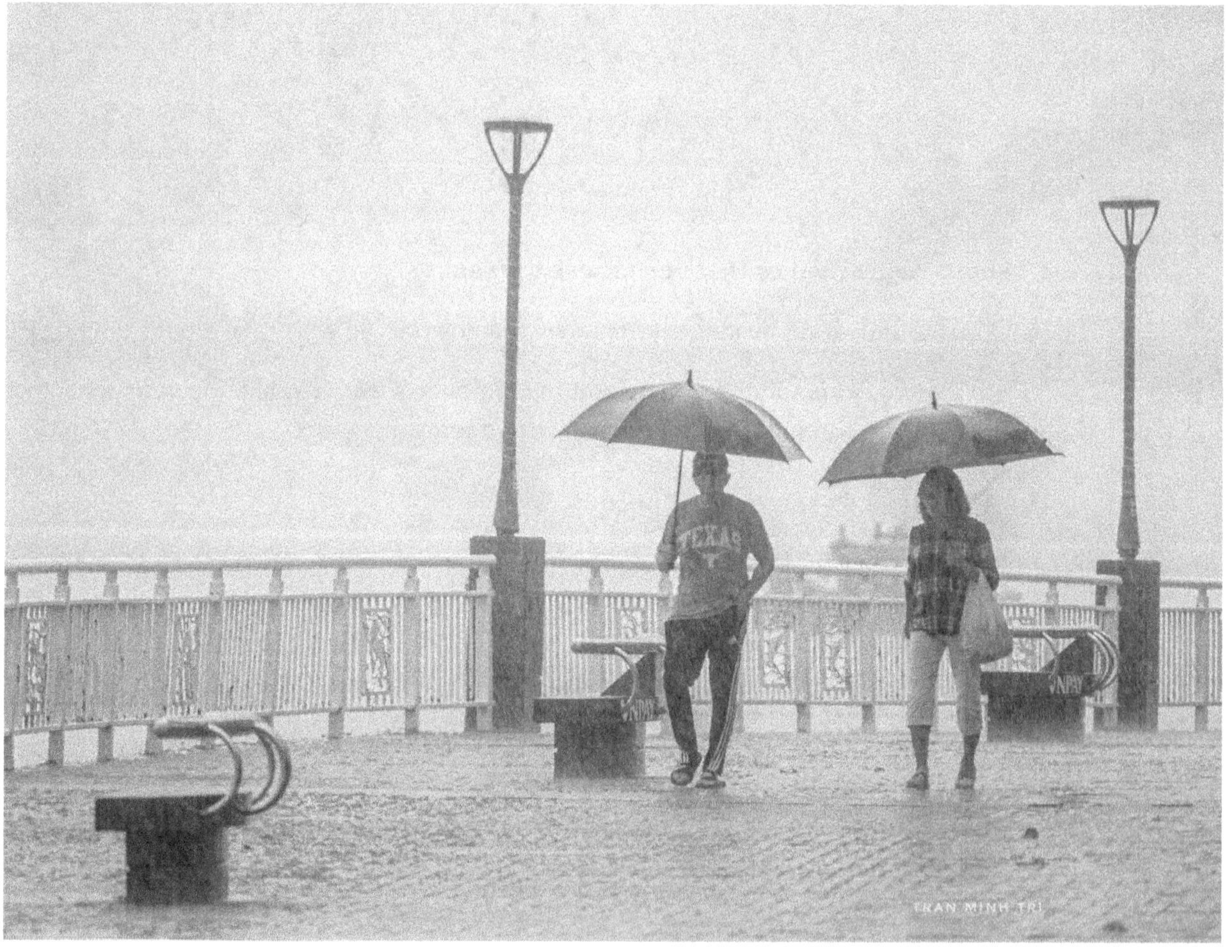

- **Minimalist photography:** Choose simple subjects and refined compositions to create minimalist photos that are evocative and artistic.

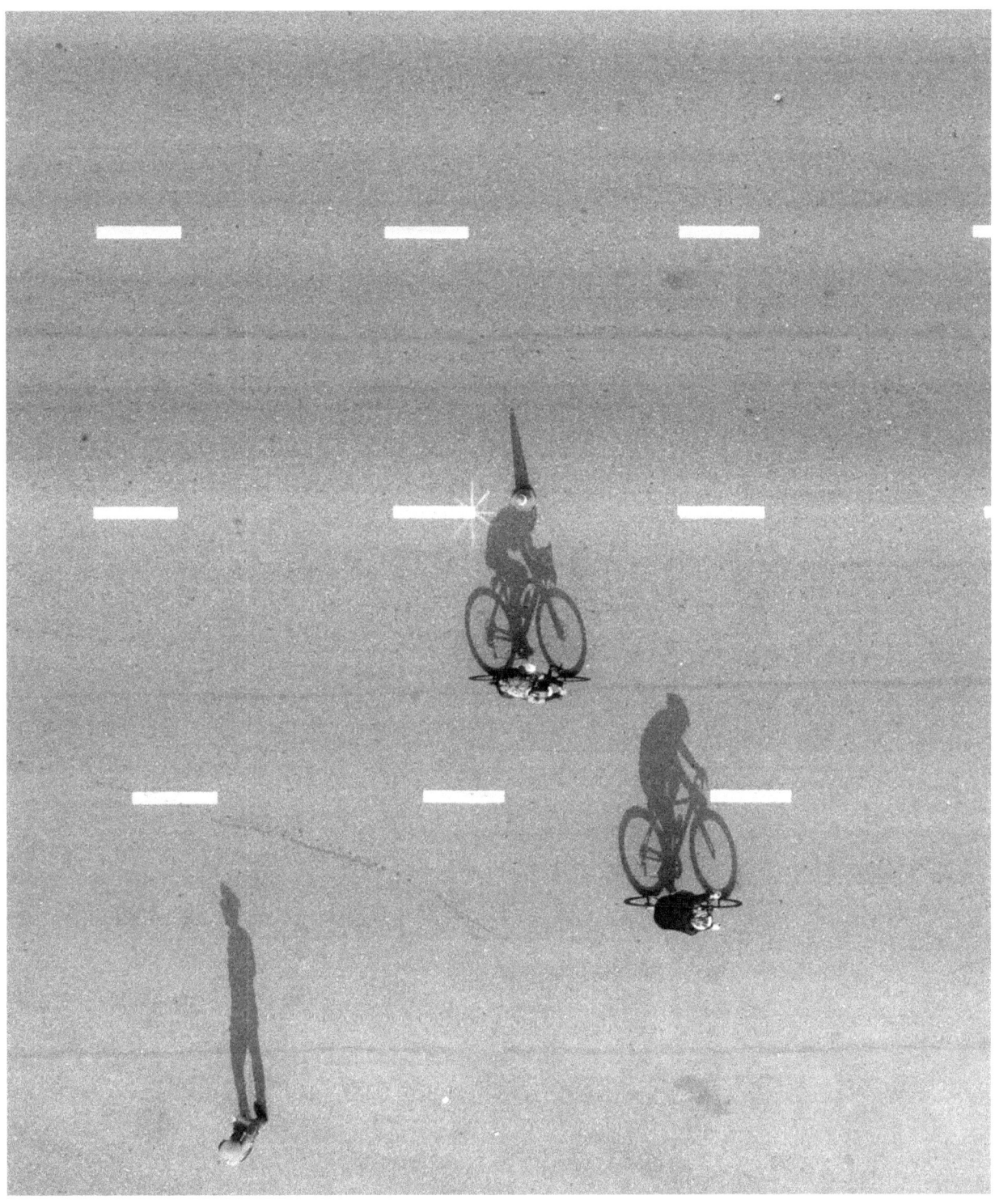

Step outside, observe, feel, and "hunt" for those beautiful moments. You'll be amazed to discover how diverse and inspiring the world around you truly is!

Part 2: Budget-Friendly Photography Techniques

Chapter 4: Mastering Natural Light

Light is the most crucial element in photography. It can bring life, magic, and emotion to your images. And the best part is, natural light is readily available, free of charge, just waiting for you to explore and conquer.

4.1 Analyzing Types of Natural Light

4.1.1 Sunlight

- **Characteristics:** A powerful light source that changes throughout the day and with weather conditions.
- **Advantages:** Easily accessible, creates various lighting effects.
- **Disadvantages:** Can be difficult to control, may cause overexposure or underexposure.
- **Types of sunlight:**
    - **Direct sunlight:** Creates hard shadows and strong contrast. Suitable for landscapes and architecture.

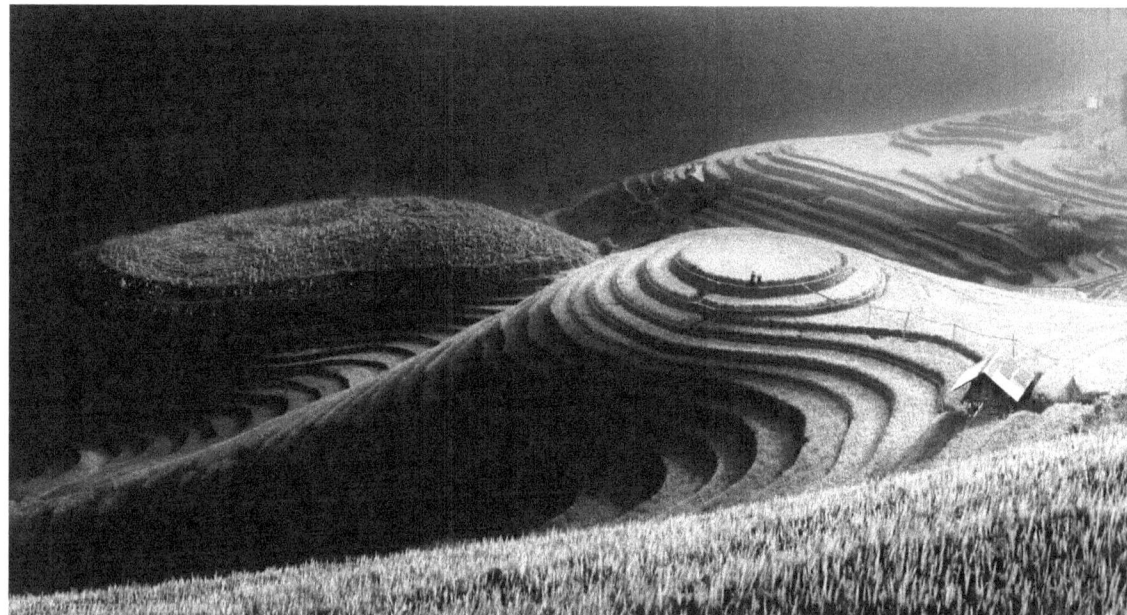

    - **Diffused sunlight:** Soft light that produces gentle shadows. Ideal for portraits and still life.

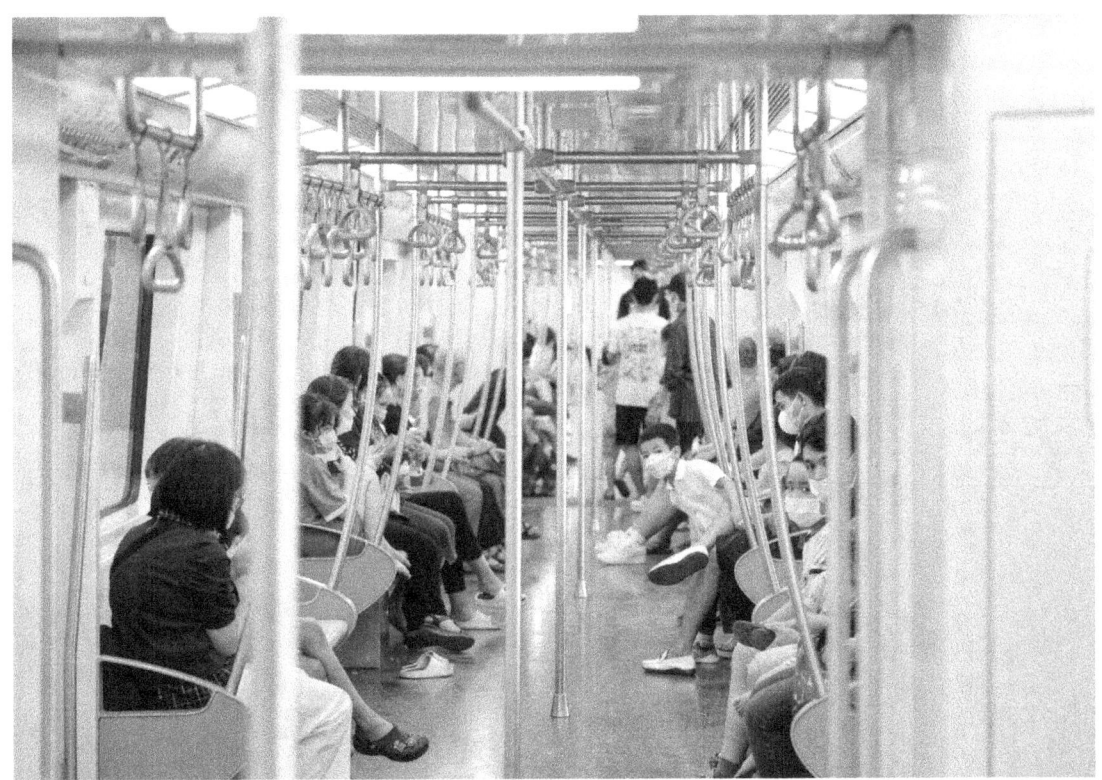

- **Backlight:** Creates a rim light effect, adding depth to the photo. Suitable for silhouettes and artistic portraits.

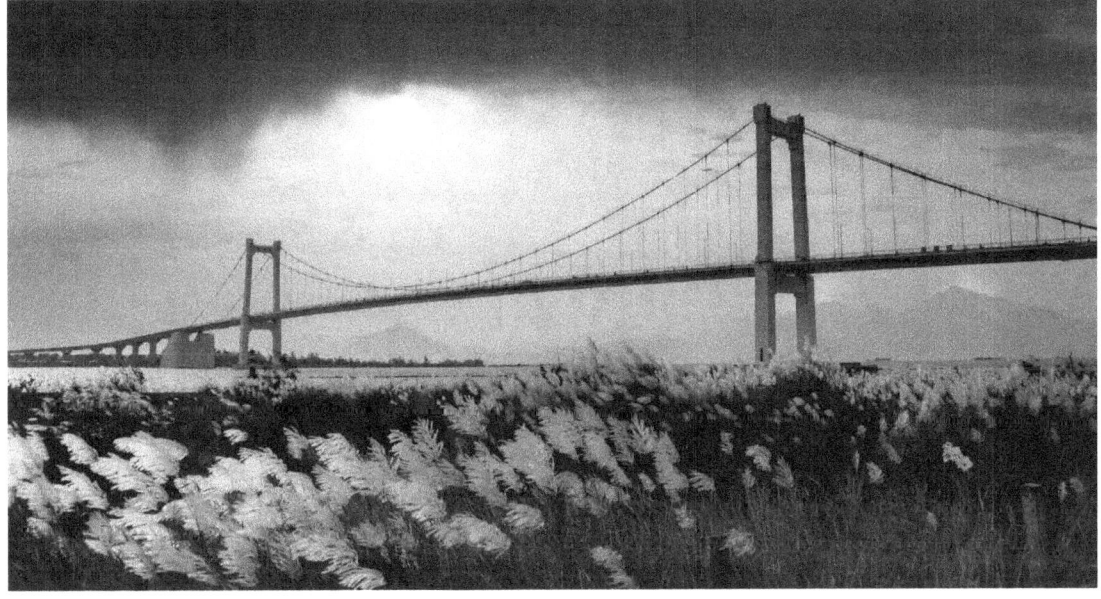

4.1.2 Indoor Light

- **Characteristics:** Weaker than sunlight, often influenced by the color of walls and objects.
- **Advantages:** More stable than sunlight, creates a cozy atmosphere.

- **Disadvantages:** Can cause noise and inaccurate colors.
- **How to utilize:** Use windows and balconies as the main light source, supplemented with artificial lighting if needed.

Indoor portrait photography with window light

4.1.3 Night Light

- **Characteristics:** Dim, often comes from streetlights, neon signs, or moonlight.
- **Advantages:** Creates a magical and romantic atmosphere.
- **Disadvantages:** Requires supporting equipment like a tripod and flash.
- **How to utilize:** Increase ISO, decrease shutter speed, and use a tripod for long exposures.

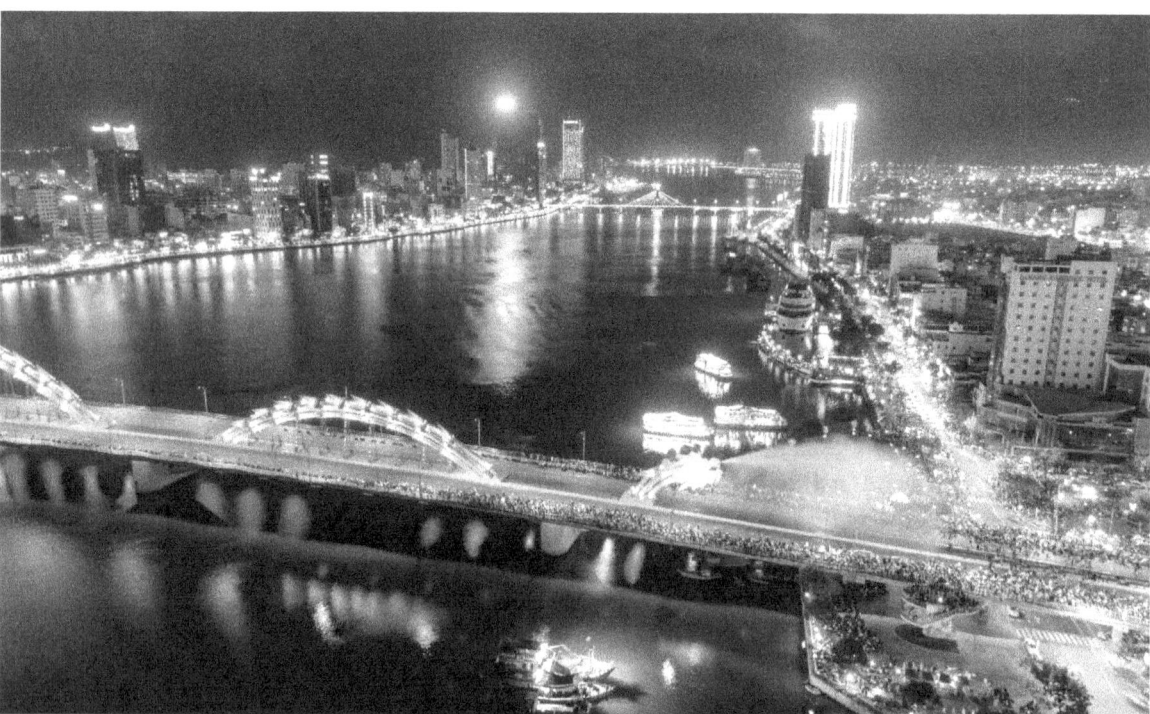

4.2 Utilizing the "Golden Hour" and "Blue Hour"

- **"Golden hour":** The short period after sunrise and before sunset. During this time, sunlight has a warm, golden hue, casting long, soft shadows, making it ideal for landscapes and portraits.

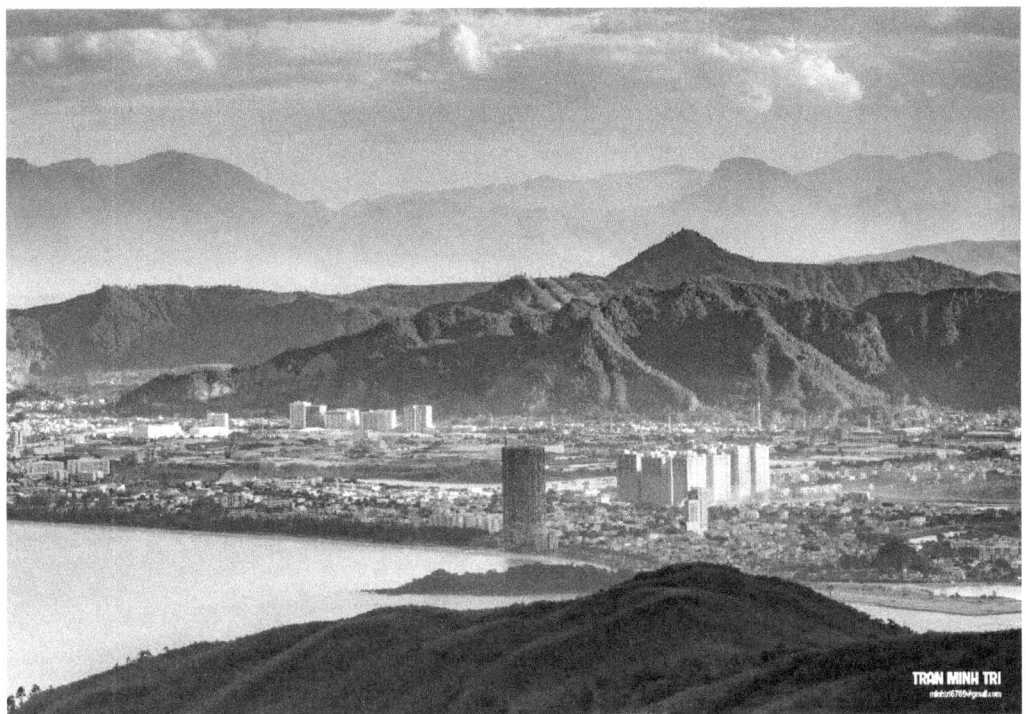

- **"Blue hour":** The short period before sunrise and after sunset. The sky takes on a deep blue color, creating a magical atmosphere, perfect for architecture and cityscapes.

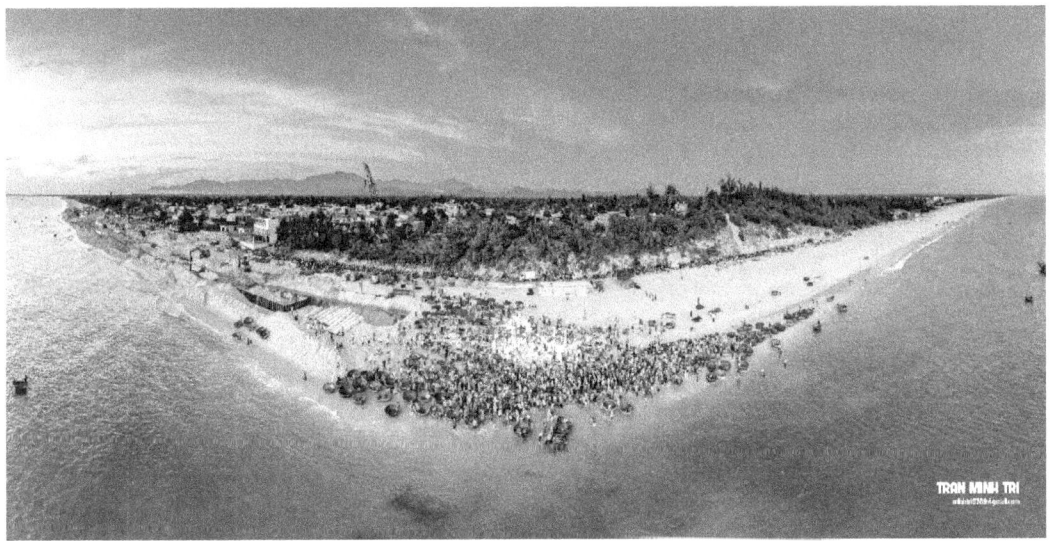

4.3 Backlight, Shadow, and Silhouette Photography

- **Backlight photography:** Positioning the subject in front of the light source creates a rim light effect, adding depth. Careful metering is necessary to avoid overexposure.
- **Shadow photography:** Utilize shadows to create striking and unique photos. Shadows can be the main subject or a complementary element in the composition.

- **Silhouette photography:** Shooting the subject against a bright background creates a dark silhouette. This technique produces dramatic, mysterious, and artistic photos.

By understanding and mastering natural light, you can create beautiful photos without the expense of artificial lighting equipment.

Chapter 5: Impressive Composition Without Expensive Lenses

Composition is the art of arranging elements within a frame to create a harmonious, engaging, and effective photograph that conveys a message. Many people mistakenly believe that only expensive lenses can produce beautiful compositions. However, the truth is that you can absolutely create stunning compositions with an ordinary camera or phone, as long as you grasp the fundamental principles and apply them creatively.

5.1 Revisiting Classic Composition Rules

- **Rule of Thirds:** Divide the frame into nine equal parts using two horizontal and two vertical lines. Place your subject at the intersections of these lines to create balance and draw attention.
- **Leading lines:** Use lines (straight or curved), fences, roads, or paths to guide the viewer's eye towards the main subject, creating depth and movement within the image.
- **Emphasis:** Highlight the main subject using contrasting colors, lighting, size, or unique positioning.

Creating emphasis with contrasting colors

- **Negative space:** Leave empty space around the subject to create a sense of spaciousness and focus attention on the main point of interest.

Utilizing negative space in still life photography

- **Symmetry:** Arrange elements symmetrically around an axis to create a sense of balance and stability.

Symmetrical composition in architecture photography

5.2 Creative Composition with Unique Angles

The shooting angle significantly impacts the composition and mood of a photograph. Experiment with different angles to create unique images:

- **Low angle:** Shooting from a low perspective creates a sense of power and grandeur for the subject. Suitable for architecture and trees.

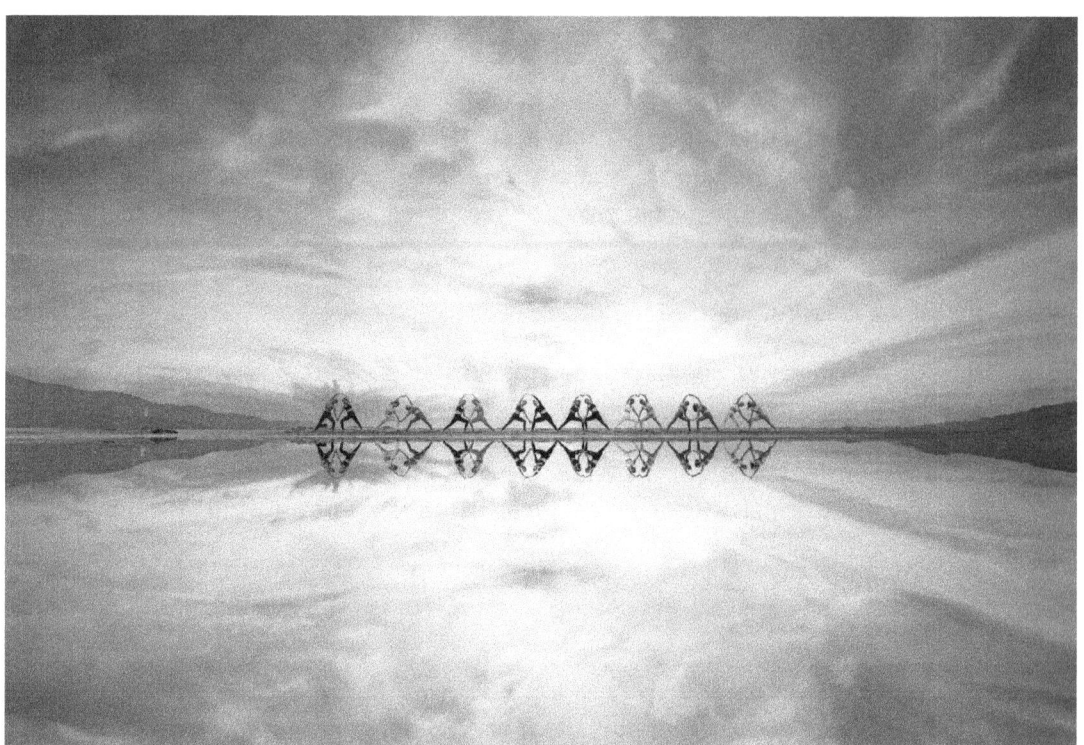

Photographing a skyscraper from a low angle

- **High angle:** Shooting from above condenses the space and creates a sense of overview. Ideal for landscapes and crowds.

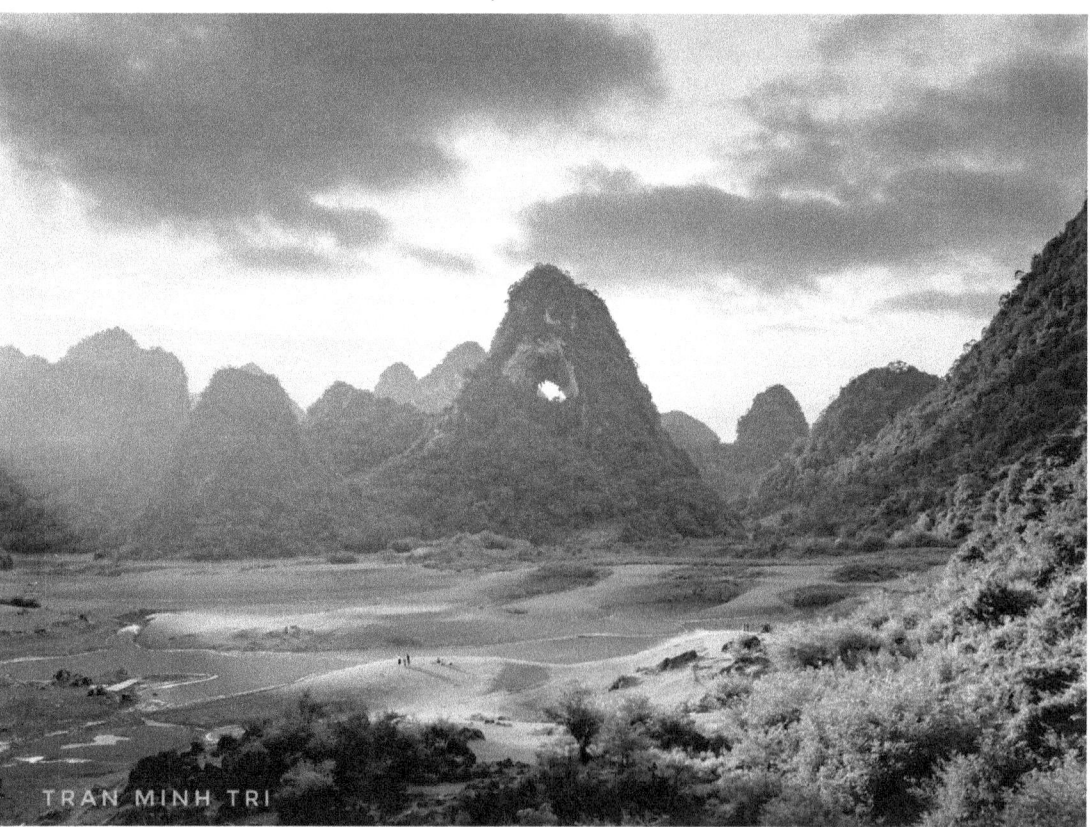

- **Tilted angle:** Creates a sense of movement, surprise, and unconventionality.

5.3 Utilizing Negative Space, Lines, and Colors for Emphasis

- **Negative space:** The empty space around the subject not only provides a sense of spaciousness but also helps to emphasize the main subject.

- **Lines:** Lines within the frame can guide the viewer's eye, creating depth and movement.

- **Color:** Employ contrasting colors, complementary colors, or a consistent color palette to create emphasis and leave a lasting impression on the viewer.

Remember, composition is not just about rules; it's also about creativity. Don't hesitate to experiment with new angles and cleverly combine elements within the frame to produce striking images that reflect your unique style.

Chapter 6: Professional Post-Processing for Free

Post-processing is a crucial step in perfecting a photograph. It allows you to fine-tune imperfections and express your creative vision. The good news is, you don't need to spend money on expensive software like Photoshop or Lightroom. Today, numerous free photo editing software options offer powerful features, enabling you to create professional-looking images without spending a dime.

6.1 Introducing Free Photo Editing Software

- **GIMP (GNU Image Manipulation Program):** A powerful, open-source software often referred to as the "free Photoshop." GIMP provides a comprehensive set of professional photo editing tools, ranging from basic to advanced. It allows you to perform simple tasks like cropping and color correction, as well as complex techniques like photo manipulation and creating special effects.
    - **Advantages:** Free, open-source, cross-platform, feature-rich.
    - **Disadvantages:** The interface can be quite complex for beginners.

    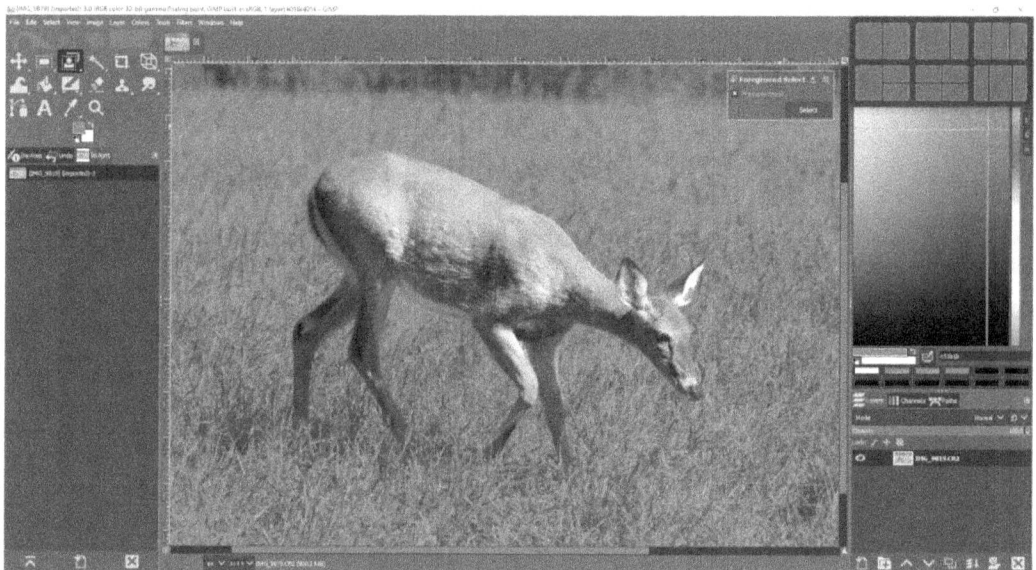

    GIMP software interface

- **Darktable:** A professional photo editing software focused on RAW image processing. Darktable offers powerful tools for adjusting colors, contrast, sharpness, and noise reduction.
    - **Advantages:** Professional-grade, excellent RAW processing, many advanced features.
    - **Disadvantages:** The interface can be quite complex, mainly geared towards experienced users.

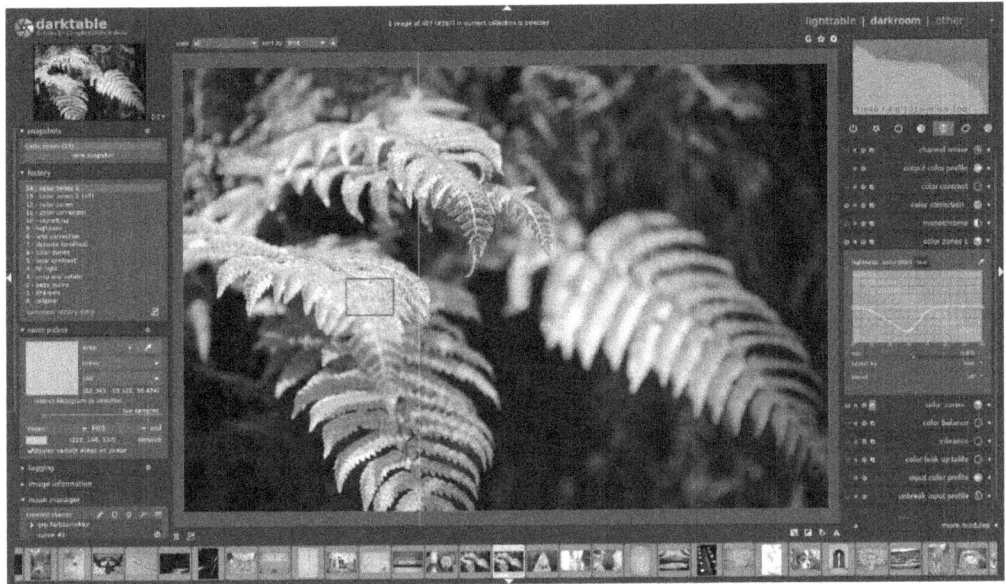

Darktable software interface

- **Snapseed:** A free photo editing app for mobile phones, developed by Google. Snapseed offers a user-friendly interface with a wide range of basic and advanced photo editing tools, along with numerous filters.

    - **Advantages:** Free, easy to use, feature-rich, various filters.

    - **Disadvantages:** Fewer advanced features compared to GIMP or Darktable.

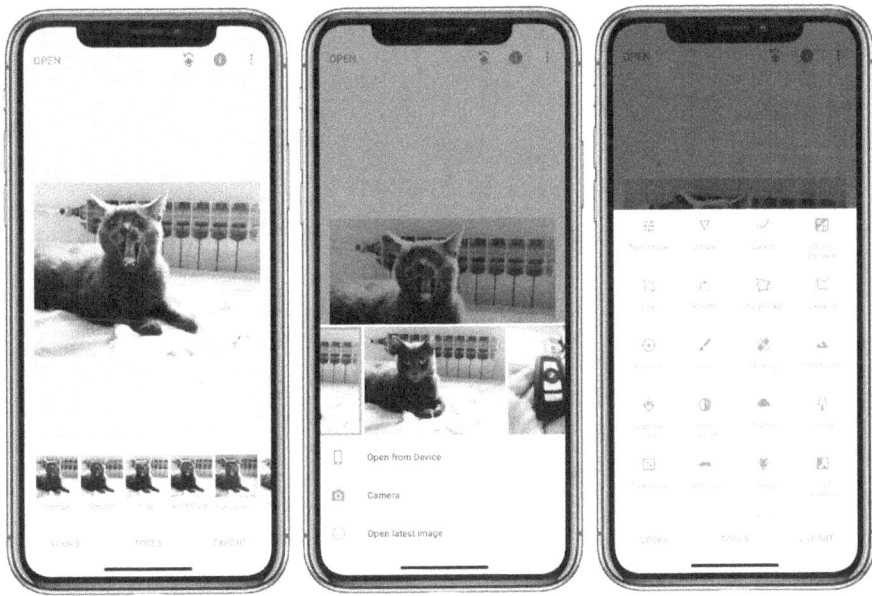

Snapseed app interface

In addition, there are many other free photo editing software and apps available, such as:

- **PhotoScape:** Simple and easy-to-use photo editing software, suitable for beginners.

- **Pixlr:** A web and mobile photo editing app that offers various tools and filters.

- **Fotor:** A web and mobile photo editing app focused on portrait retouching and creating collages.

6.2 Basic Photo Editing Techniques

- **Cropping:** Removing unwanted parts of an image, changing its size and composition.
- **White balance:** Adjusting the colors to accurately reflect the scene's true colors.
- **Contrast:** Increasing or decreasing the difference between light and dark areas in the image.
- **Brightness:** Adjusting the overall brightness of the image.
- **Sharpening:** Enhancing the clarity and detail of the image.
- **Noise reduction:** Removing noise or grain, often present in images captured in low light or with a high ISO setting.

6.3 Creating Unique Photo Effects with Free Tools

Free photo editing software and apps provide various tools to create unique effects:

- **Color effects:** Changing the color palette, creating vintage, retro, or film-like effects.
- **Light effects:** Adding lens flares, bokeh, or sunlight effects.
- **Texture effects:** Applying textures to create a classic or nostalgic feel.
- **Lomo effects:** Creating vignettes, color shifts, and replicating the look of photos taken with Lomo cameras.

Take advantage of free photo editing software and apps to enhance your images and express your creativity in every shot.

Chapter 8: Free Online Resources for Photographers

The internet is a vast treasure trove of knowledge, and for photography enthusiasts, there are countless free online resources to learn, improve skills, and connect with the community. This chapter will introduce you to helpful websites, blogs, forums, stock photo platforms, and online photography communities, enabling you to "level up" your photography without spending any money.

8.1 Websites, Blogs, and Forums for Photography Knowledge and Techniques

- **Websites for learning photography:**
    - **Digital Photography School:** Offers articles and tutorials on various photography topics, from basic to advanced, suitable for both beginners and professionals.
    - **Photofocus:** Shares knowledge and experience from leading photography experts, along with equipment reviews and photo editing software tutorials.
    - **The Photo Argus:** Provides detailed tutorials on photography techniques, camera and lens usage, and photo editing software.
    - **Vua nhiếp ảnh:** A Vietnamese photography website with numerous quality articles on techniques, genres, and the art of photography.

- **Photography blogs:**
    - **Petapixel:** A popular photography blog featuring interesting news and articles about photography and technology.
    - **Fstoppers:** A blog sharing experiences and tips from professional photographers.
    - **DIY Photography:** A blog dedicated to budget-friendly photography tips, tricks, and DIY accessories.

- **Photography forums:**
    - **Flickr:** The world's largest platform for sharing photos and discussing photography.
    - **500px:** An online photography community where you can share your work, receive feedback, and learn from other photographers.
    - **VNPhoto:** The largest photography forum in Vietnam, a place for exchanging and sharing experiences within the Vietnamese photography community.

8.2 Free Stock Photo Platforms

Need stock photos for content creation, design, or learning materials? Check out these free stock photo platforms:

- **Unsplash:** Offers millions of high-quality, free images across diverse themes.
- **Pixabay:** A free stock photo platform with a vast library of images, vectors, and videos.
- **Pexels:** Provides high-quality, carefully curated free stock photos.
- **Burst:** A free stock photo platform from Shopify, focusing on business and e-commerce themes.

8.3 Online Photography Communities for Learning and Networking

Joining online photography communities is a great way to connect with like-minded individuals, learn from their experiences, receive feedback on your work, and explore collaboration opportunities.

- **Facebook groups:** There are numerous active Facebook groups dedicated to photography, such as "Hội nhiếp ảnh Việt Nam," "Nhiếp ảnh cho người mới bắt đầu," and "Cộng đồng nhiếp ảnh Sài Gòn."

- **Instagram:** Follow your favorite photographers and participate in photography contests on Instagram to connect and learn.

- **Meetup:** Find photography meetups and workshops in your area to meet and interact with other photographers in person.

Take advantage of these free online resources to nurture your passion for photography, develop your skills, and expand your network within the photography community.

Conclusion: Photography is for Sharing

On your journey exploring the colorful world of photography, you might have been overwhelmed by expensive equipment, "big" lenses, and advanced technologies. But remember, photography is not a "gear" race. The true value of a photograph lies in the emotions, stories, and messages it conveys.

Whether simple or modern, a camera is just a tool. The important thing is the "photographer" behind the lens – that's you – with your vision, creativity, and passion. Explore the potential of your existing equipment, utilize light, composition, and shooting angles, and don't forget to hone your post-processing skills.

The world around us is filled with beautiful moments and stories waiting to be told. Open your "photographer's eye," observe, feel, and create to capture those moments in your unique style.

Don't hesitate to practice, experiment, and share your work with the world. Each photo is a story, an emotion, a unique perspective you want to convey. And who knows, perhaps the works created with simple equipment will inspire those around you.

Let photography become your language, a means to share emotions and connect with the world.

www.ingramcontent.com/pod-product-compliance
Lightning Source LLC
Chambersburg PA
CBHW081021240526
45471CB00018B/3939